W9-AZU-369

My Cat's Not Fat, He's Just Big-Boned

FALL to YOUR KNEES.

CAT ADORATION DAY.

OTHER BOOKS BY
NICOLE HOLLANDER

I'm in Training to Be Tall and Blonde

Ma, Can I Be A Feminist and Still Like Men?

That Woman Must Be on Drugs

Mercy, It's the Revolution and I'm in My Bathrobe

My Weight Is Always Perfect for My Height—Which Varies

Hi, This Is Sylvia

Sylvia on Sundays

Okay, Thinner Thighs for Everyone

Never Take Your Cat to a Salad Bar

The Whole Enchilada

Tales From the Planet Sylvia

You Can't Take it With You, So Eat it Now

Everything Here is Mine

Female Problems: An Unhelpful Guide

My Cat's Not Fat, He's Just Big-Boned

by Nicole Hollander

A Division of Sourcebooks

Naperville, IL • Bridgeport, CT

Copyright ©1998 by Nicole Hollander

All rights reserved. No part of this book may be reproduced in any form or
by any electronic or mechanical means including information storage and
retrieval systems—except in the case of brief quotations embodied in critical
articles or reviews—without permission in writing from its publisher,
Hysteria Publications (an imprint of Sourcebooks).

 Hysteria Publications, a division of Sourcebooks, Inc.

Naperville Office	Bridgeport Office
P.O. Box 4410	P.O. Box 38581
Naperville, IL 60567-4410	Bridgeport, CT 06605
630.961.3900	203.333.9399
630-961-2168 fax	203.367.7188 fax

Cover and interior design: Tom Greensfelder Design

Printed and bound in the United States of America
BG 10 9 8 7 6 5 4 3

ISBN 1-887166-43-2

this book is dedicated to
Eric, IZZY And Buddy...
as BiG as they wanna Be.

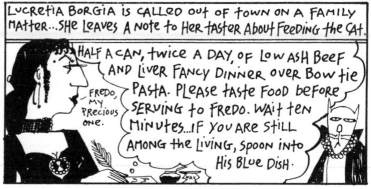

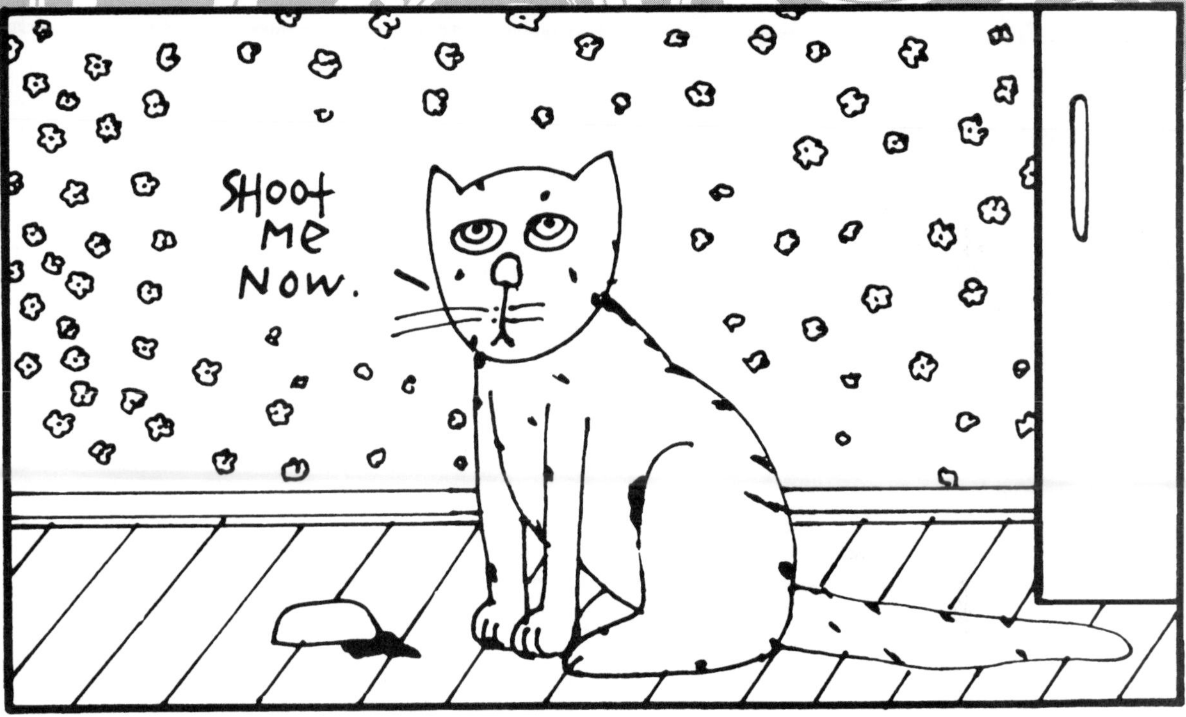
SHOOT ME NOW.

CATS WHO HYPNOTIZE DOGS

YOU WILL SLEEP NOW AND WHEN YOU AWAKEN YOU WILL BE UNABLE TO COME WHEN YOUR MASTER CALLS BECAUSE OF AN IRRESTIBLE URGE TO STUDY A SPOT ON THE WALL THAT LOOKS LIKE THAT STUFF THAT LOOKS LIKE BACON TO DOGS.

FROM THE BOOK OF HEROIC CATS

ON EASTER I DISGUISED MYSELF AS A BUNNY TO KEEP TABS ON MY MISTRESS'S SLIMY SWAIN. HUNDREDS OF CHILDREN WERE GAMBOLING ON THE LAWN... PART OF OUR ANNUAL EGG-ROLLING PARTY... SO I WAS ALREADY QUITE CRANKY WHEN I SPIED HER SMARMY SWEETHEART SELECTING EGGS MARKED WITH A TINY RED "P," POISON! AND PUTTING THEM IN HER EASTER BASKET. NO TIME TO GRIND MY TEETH. I SPED ACROSS THE LAWN, SCATTERING CHILDREN, EGGS AND THE OCCASIONAL BIRD IN MY WAKE. I RUSHED HIM OFF HIS FEET, INTO THE PUNCH BOWL. SHE PRETENDED TO BE MIFFED, BUT LATER WHISPERED: "WELL DONE, DRAGONSLAYER!"

OUR HAPPINESS is their WHOLE LIFE.

SHE BOUGHT ME this AQUARIUM VIDEO-TAPE. I'VE GOT A GOOD HEART. I GO UP TO THE T.V. SET, I PAW THE SCREEN PRETENDING I'M TRYING TO CATCH THE FISH, I MAKE FELINE HUNTING SOUNDS. IF THERE'S A KITTY HEAVEN, I'M IN.

HE'S SO CUTE, HE WATCHES THAT VIDEO FOR HOURS.

A CAT COMPLAINS ABOUT CRUEL CAT OWNERS.

THEY NAMED ME "SEX MACHINE." YOU KNOW, AFTER THE JAMES BROWN SONG, SORT OF A JOKE AT MY EXPENSE, RIGHT? SO WHEN I HAVE TO GO TO THE VET AND SHE ASKS MY NAME THEY LOSE THEIR NERVE... THEY TELL HER: "FRISKY." IT ISN'T ENOUGH I HAVE TO GO TO THE VET, I HAVE TO HAVE AN IDENTITY CRISIS TOO? I COULD SPIT.

23

HEARTBREAKING COMPLAINTS OF CATS

She sees a cat on the street and she has to bring it home. Some of them were probably just out taking a walk. We have seven cats now. That's the give away... normal people never have an odd number of cats.

Oh Edgar, guess what followed me home.

Panel 1: GOOD MORNING, BOYS. WHAT'S UP? / WE HAD OUR ASTROLOGICAL CHARTS DONE. / BAD NEWS...

Panel 2: EXCUSE ME? / WE WOULD BE MORE COMPATIBLE... / WITH CINDY CRAWFORD.

Panel 3: I'LL CALL HER... SEE IF SHE'D LIKE TO SEND HER HUSBAND OVER IN EXCHANGE. / IF SHE'S NOT HOME... / TRY CLAUDIA SCHIFFER.

FROM the MEMOIRS OF AN HEROIC Feline...

"I SPIED HER SO-CALLED HUSBAND SLIPPING A SUSPICIOUS SUBSTANCE INTO THE GARLIC BUTTER... I WATCHED AS HE SET IT BEFORE HER WITH A FLOURISH AND A SMILE OF SMUG SATISFACTION... SHE DIPPED HER ESCARGOT AND BROUGHT IT UP TO HER SWEET LIPS. NO TIME TO LOSE... I SKIDDED ACROSS THE TABLE AND KICKPLACED THE SAUCE INTO SPACE... BUTTER AND ESCARGOT EVERYWHERE! I RETREATED. AS SHE LEFT THE ROOM TO GET THE MOP AND PAIL, SHE WHISPERED IN MY EAR: "MERCI, MON CAPITAINE."

CATS WITH SHORT ATTENTION SPANS

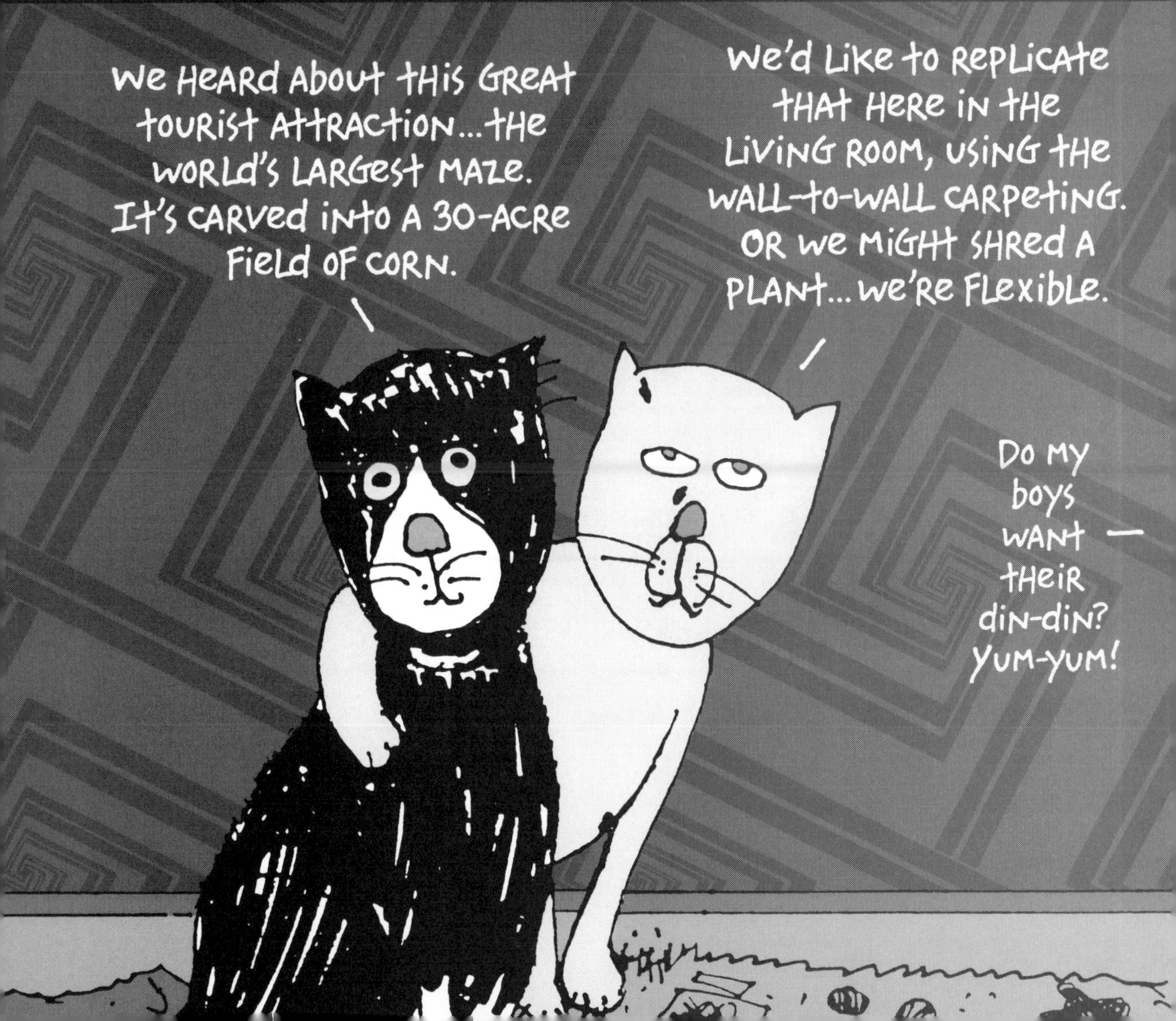

this is your CAT'S BRAIN ON CATNIP.

I FiND the study oF BiRDS FASCiNATiNG. HoW ReWARDiNG to observe their FLiGHt PATterNs, NestiNG AND FeeDiNG HAbits, the trAiNiNG oF their YouNG, the beHAVioR oF MALes AND FeMALes... AND, oF course, they're Quite YuMMY.

CATS IN CRISIS

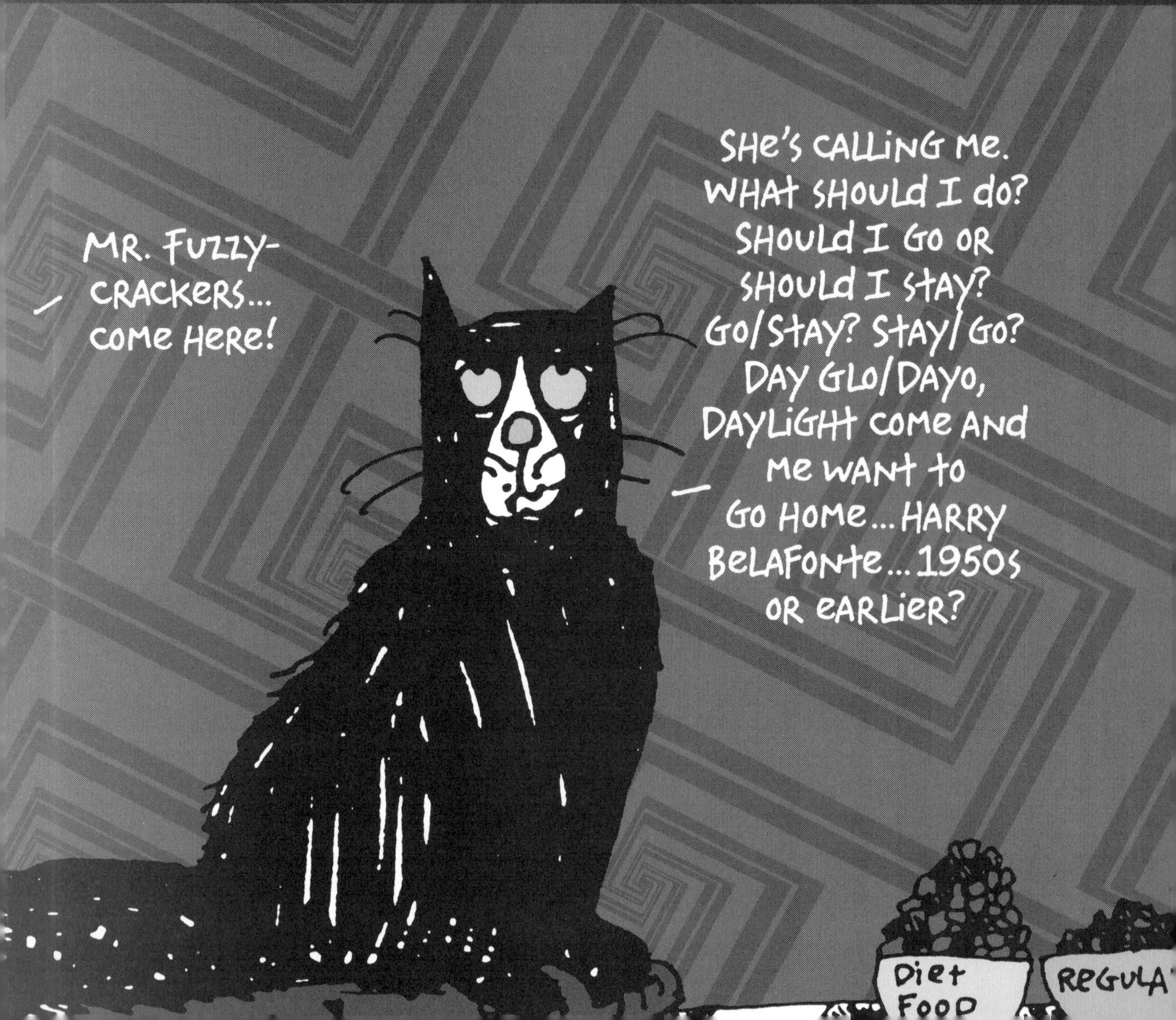

Does she ever ask me if I can stand to hear Patsy Cline fall to pieces one more time? Whine, whine, whine. It puts me off my feed.
I fall to pieces, each time I see you again...
CHAT

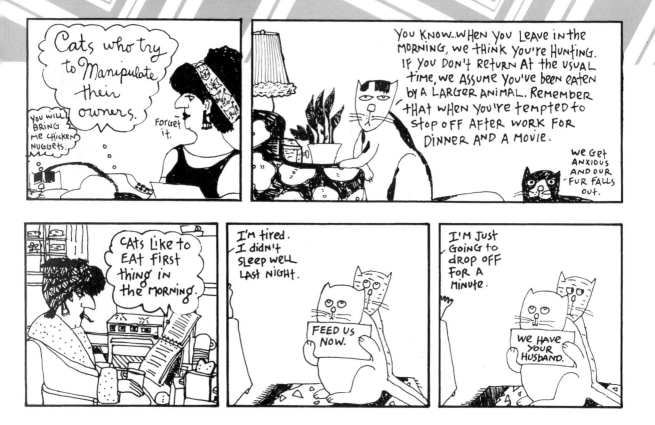

RASHOMON FOR CATS

I WANT TO GO OUTSIDE. I WANT TO ROAM FREE, FEEL THE WIND IN MY HAIR... birds in MY teeth.

BUT SHE KEEPS ME A PRISONER HERE, AGAINST MY NATURE.

I LET HER OUT IN THE BACKYARD ONCE, BUT A LEAF FELL ON HER AND SHE HID UNDER the COUCH FOR A WEEK.

TERRIBLY MEAN CAT LIES.

WHERE ARE MY LENSES?

I'M SURE I DON'T KNOW. I HAVE NO USE FOR GREEN CONTACT LENSES. MY EYES ARE NATURALLY GREEN. I'M NOT THE ONE WITH THE WASHED OUT BABY-BLUES. HAVE YOU LOOKED IN YOUR HANDBAG? YOU COULD LOSE A STATION WAGON IN THERE.

51

Dear Foolish in Fresno, Give the ring BACK AT ONCE. there Are plenty of nice Men out there, MEN WHO CARRY PHOTOGRAPHS of their CATS in their WALLets... Next time you Go out with A GUY, Ask to see His WALLet. AND ANother THING: if He's ALLeRGic to CATS He'LL be ALLeRGic to SOMethiNG else, Like ALL your old FrieNDS.

A CAT ~ HeLp & ~ LoviNG THAT MAN OF MiNe...

54

CATS ARE MORE RESISTANT TO HAVING THEIR TEETH BRUSHED THAN DOGS, BUT TRICKS CAN BE USED.

SHE WALKS TOWARD ME. HER RIGHT HAND IS WRAPPED IN A CLOTH THAT SMELLS LIKE IT'S BEEN DIPPED IN CLAM JUICE. I SWEAR I HAD NO IDEA THAT SHE WANTED TO CLEAN MY TEETH. I DIDN'T KNOW WHAT SHE WAS GOING TO DO. IT SEEMED KINKY TO ME, SO I BIT HER.

WHEN YOU NEED DENTURES, DON'T COME WHINING TO ME.

PHIL

A CAT SUFFERS FALLOUT FROM THE WAR ON DRUGS

SO SHE SAYS I CAN'T HAVE CATNIP ANY MORE BECAUSE IT'S LIKE A DRUG. SO, LIKE, WHAT'S SHE WORRIED ABOUT: I'M NOT GOING TO DO WELL IN SCHOOL OR WHAT?

EDGAR, come AND meet the puppy I bought to keep you COMPANY.

the word "Betrayal" Leaps to mind, but doesn't quite conjure up the Full Horror of what has occurred Here today.

CRUEL CATS WITH SPECIAL TALENTS

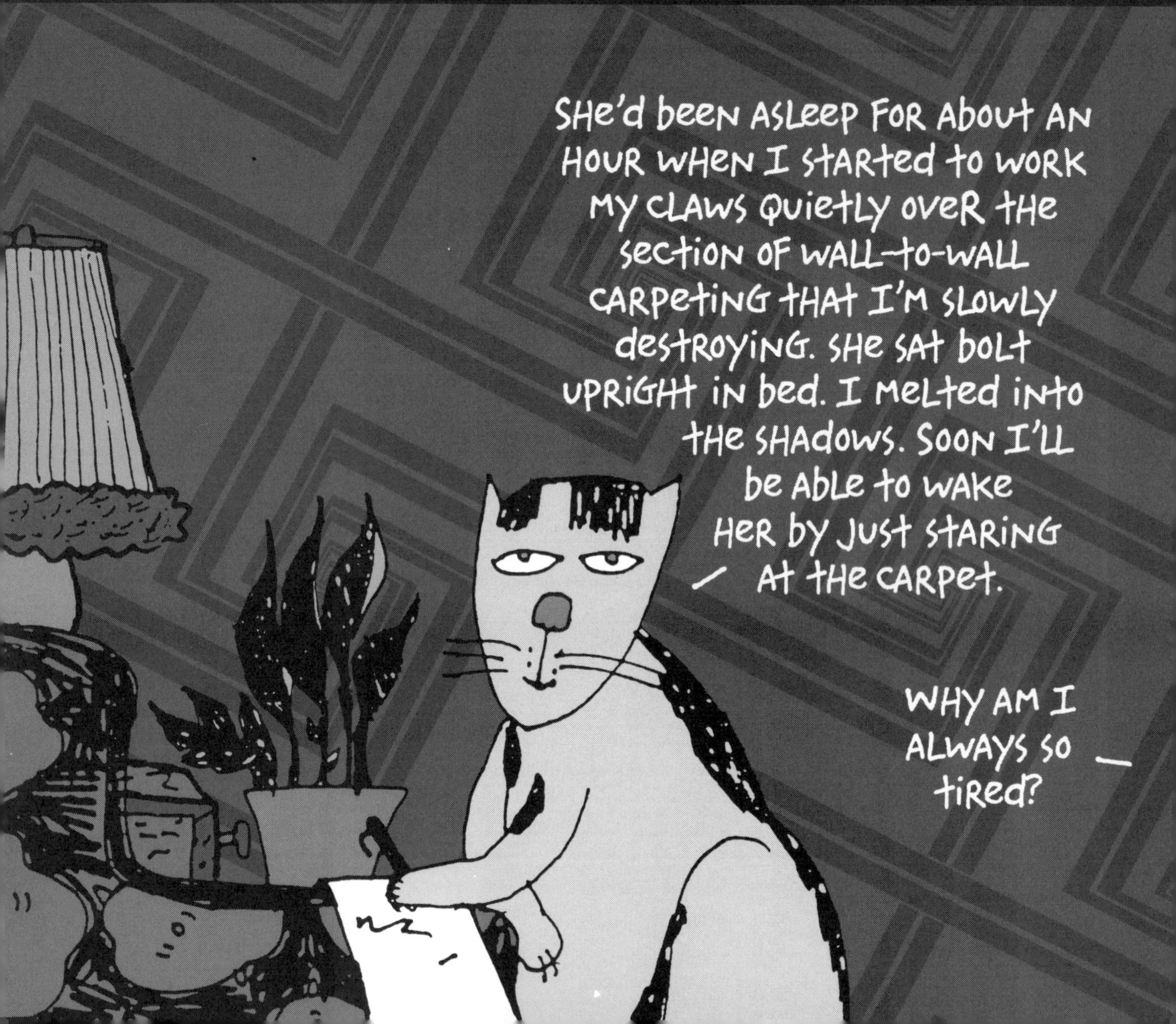

CATS LIKE YOU TO COME HOME RIGHT AFTER WORK.

AFTER WORK WE'RE GOING TO HAVE DINNER AND SEE THAT NEW PLAY EVERYONE'S TALKING ABOUT... I HAVEN'T HAD A NIGHT OUT IN AGES. I'M SO EXCITED.

YOU WILL SLEEP NOW, AND WHEN YOU AWAKEN, YOU WILL HAVE NO MEMORY OF MY INSTRUCTIONS... BUT TONIGHT, AS THE CURTAIN RISES, YOU WILL HURRY FROM THE THEATER, STOPPING ONLY TO PURCHASE A CAN OF TUNA, WHICH YOU WILL STUFF INTO YOUR TINY EVENING BAG AND BRING TO ME.

CATS SPEAK OUT ON MUSIC.

WE FIND THE HUMAN SINGING VOICE SOMEWHAT UNPLEASANT. OF COURSE, THERE'S NOT MUCH WE CAN DO ABOUT THAT NOW.

HUMANS LISTEN TO MANY DIFFERENT KINDS OF MUSIC. THAT'S WHY THEY'RE SO STRESSED OUT.

WHEN CATS RULE THE WORLD, EVERYONE WILL LISTEN EXCLUSIVELY TO GERSHWIN... MAYBE A LITTLE COLE PORTER.

OH NO, THEY CAT TAKE THAT AWAY FROM ME.

67

A CAT WEIGHS HIS OPTIONS

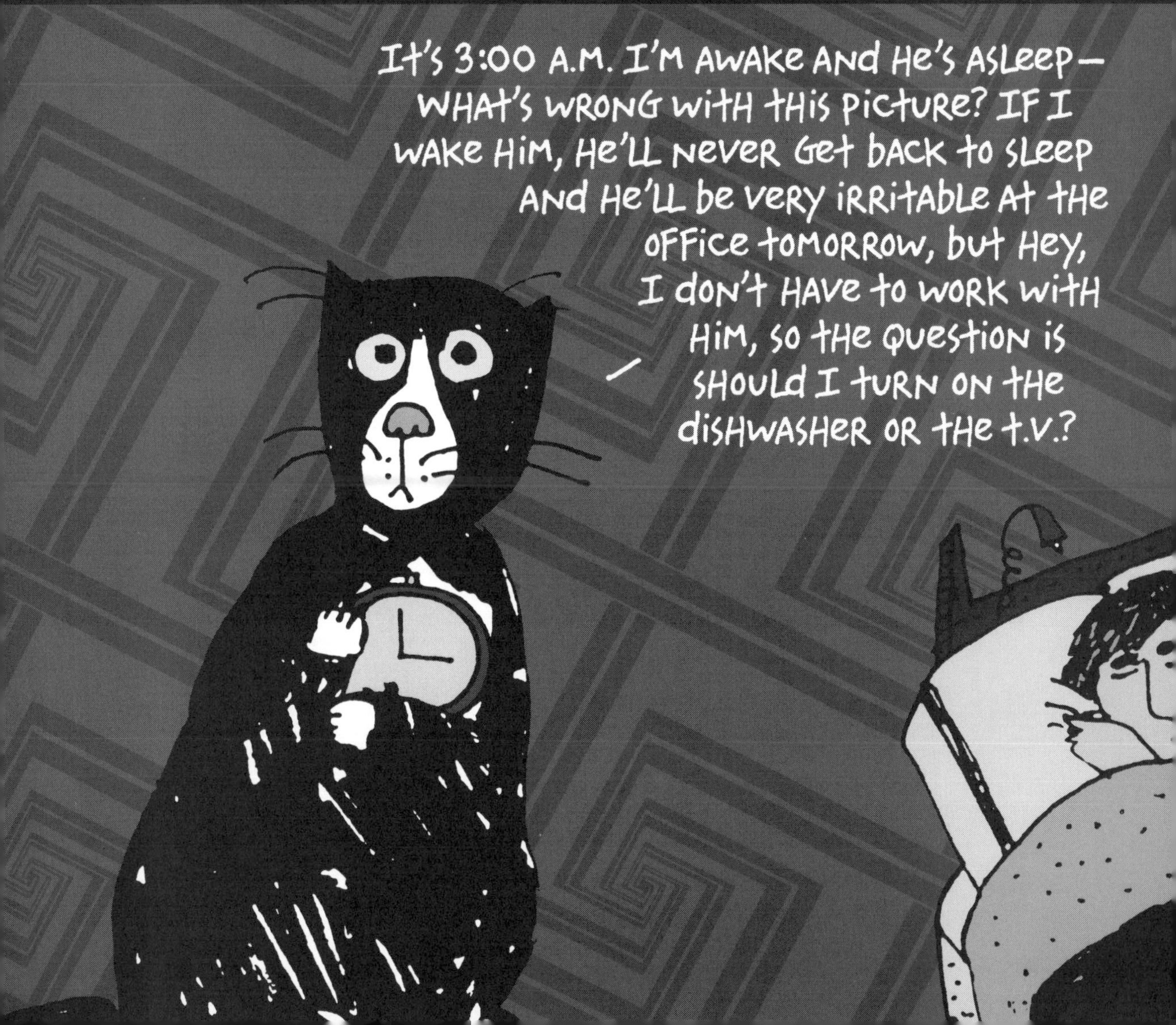

A Cat Therapist Responds

Going to the vet combines several activities that are traumatic for cats: leaving the house, riding in a moving metal deathtrap, and being touched by a stranger who smells like a dog. the humane solution is to have the vet come to the house, no matter what it costs.

My boyfriend's best friend is allergic to cats. I read that if you wash a cat once a month, it reduces the allergen produced by the cat's oil glands.

Her cats respond

Happy to cooperate.

Eager to please.

One stipulation...

Your boyfriend joins us in the tub.

A cat discusses the new "Lite" cat foods.

I have only two pleasures in life, standing on the newspaper while you're trying to read it, and eating. Leave my food alone. If I need a kitty by-pass, I'll pay for it myself.

PLEASANT DREAMS OF BAD CATS

the Shedd Aquarium in Chicago recently identified A new species of Fish... Related to the AFRICAN cichLid. It's virtually extinct in the wild And they HAVEN'T even NAMED it yet. I dReAMT I Ate it.

WOKE UP AT 3:00 A.M. this MORNING. MANAGED to DRAG the RALPH LAUREN "RUSSIA" COLLECTION BED LINENS, the CAVALRY twill THROW WITH FAUX PERSIAN LAMB EDGING, AND SOME OF THOSE RUFFLED PILLOWS OUT OF the GUEST BEDROOM AND into the KITTY LITTER.... SO EXHAUSTED I BARELY MANAGED to STUFF the CUT-VELVET DUVET into the AQUARIUM BEFORE I FELL ASLEEP.

the PROBLEM AS SHE SEES it

At 3:00 A.M. He starts knocking stuff off the dresser. He stands on my chest. I'm at my wit's end. I don't get any sleep. He's driving me crazy.

the CAT's POINT OF VIEW.

I'M AWAKE At 3:00 A.M...

WHAT AM I supposed to do, read a book?

A CAT therapist Speaks:

Adapt to your cat's schedule. If you go to sleep earlier— SAY, right after work, you'll find yourself rarin' to go At 3:00 A.M.

the Kitty Olympics

We started slowly, kicking a small amount of litter onto the floor near the box. During the week we subtly increased the amount until...

there was as much on the floor as there was in the box. Now we're going for distance.

TWO CATS ENCOUNTER TECHNOLOGY

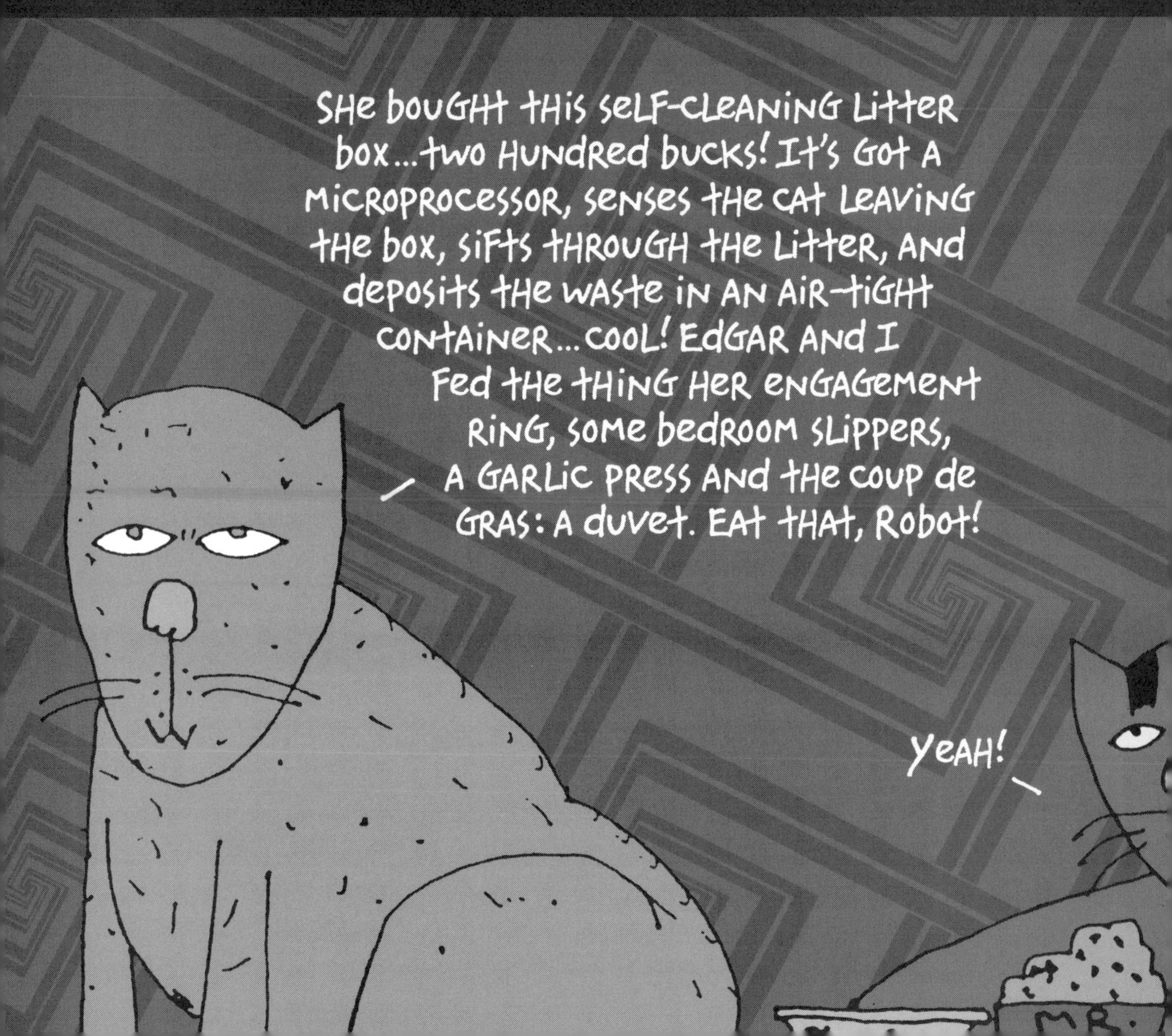

I JUST ADOPTED TWO CATS. I HAVE NO INTENTION OF CHANGING MY LIFE BECAUSE I HAVE CATS. NAVY BLUE IS MY COLOR. ALL MY CLOTHES ARE DARK BLUE, AS ARE MY LINENS, MY CARPETING AND MY COUCH.
ON THE OTHER HAND, I COULD BE COMPLETELY NUTS.
HI, GUYS. WHAT'S SHAKING?
WE COULDN'T HAVE DONE IT...
DON'T BLAME US.
WHAT HAVE YOU DONE?
OUR BRAINS ARE TOO SMALL.
SCIENTIFIC FACT.
JUST TELL ME.
THE DOG IS ON A PLANE...
TO BOGOTA.

CATS WHO HYPNOTIZE THEIR OWNERS

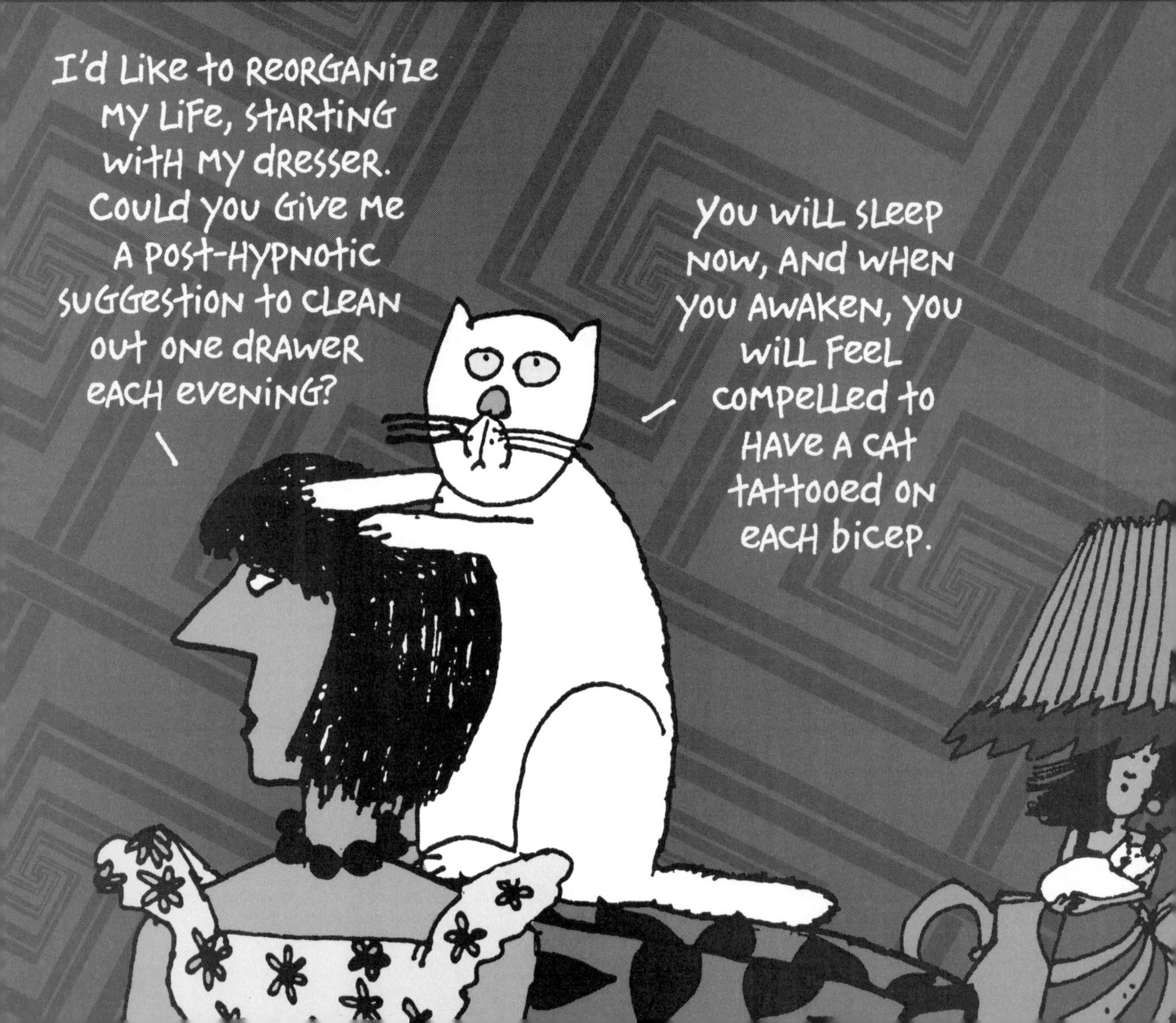

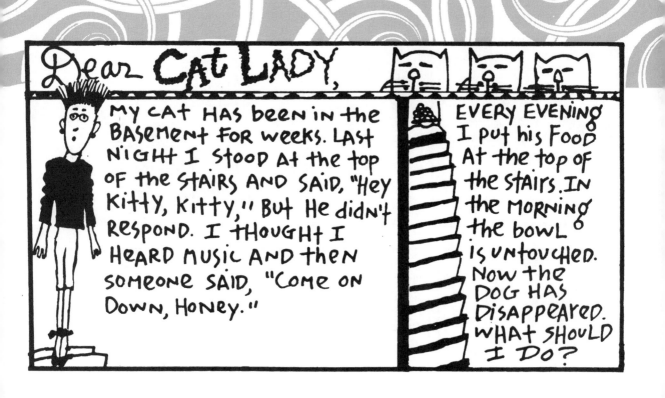

Dear CAT LADY,

MY CAT HAS been in the BASEMENT FOR weeks. LAST NIGHT I STOOD AT the top OF the STAIRS AND SAID, "Hey kitty, kitty," BUt He didn't RESPOND. I tHOUGHt I HEARD MUSIC AND THEN SOMEONE SAID, "COME ON DOWN, HONEY."

EVERY EVENING I put his FOOD At the top of the STAIRS. IN the MORNING the bowL is UNTOUCHED. NOW the DOG HAS DISAPPEARED. WHAt SHOULD I DO?

Dear Creeped-out in Cincinnati,
BRICK UP the BASEMENT.
the Cat Lady

95

97

A tiny Selection of
Dog Cartoons.

WHY?

WHEN the Ancients went out of town.

Dear Achilles, Please feed Euripides and Sally in my absence. As you may recall, Ripy likes those tiny Hot dogs and Sally must have fresh Sardines or she has a tendency to nip at one's heels. Much thanks, ta, ta... Love, Helen

the Dogs from Hell hope to lure some special PLAYMATES to their Apartment.

Free Assault WEAPONS! Free BEER! Step Inside.

WELCOME

I see one coming.

I'LL GET THE ANTLERS.

THE DOGS FROM HELL attempt to lure members of the loyal opposition to their condo.

Republicans sweep Congress!

Republicans win big!

Pre-Election Celebration! ALL Welcome! Speeches, PAC money, Prizes, Gloating... INDOOR GOLF!

Anyone coming?

Four guys with tiny flags in their lapels... Get the condiments!

the Fourth Dog

BY SYLVIA LAKE

I pulled the anonymous letter out of the tiny dog's mouth. It said: "I know what happened to your Aunt Julia at Hoover Dam...

"If you want this to remain our secret, give the dog a cashier's check for $10,000 and a biscuit." I examined the message closely. The letters seemed to have been cut from back issues of the London Times and the New York Post. That rang a bell....

The Woman who does Everything More Beautifully than you has more adorable pets than you do.

suzi

LORD JEFF

yeats

TUESDAY: RICHARD AVEDON CALLED THIS MORNING. He's terribly eager to photograph Suzi, LORD JEFF AND YEATS FOR A book He's doing on spirited yet well-behaved animals...Annie Leibovitz called as well... Mick and the Stones want to do an album cover with "S," "LJ," and "Y." I said I was sure they'd be delighted, but secretly I think they would prefer a Michael Bolton album.

the Dogs from HELL Love to PARTY.

DIDN'T GET ENOUGH PARTYING LAST NIGHT?

Looking for the ULTIMATE PARTY THRILL?

Free everything inside

Anyone coming?

Six pairs of bloodshot eyes, wearing party hats.

the **Dogs** from **HELL** try to entice some corporate playmates to their APARTMENT.

FREE FAX, Scones, CAPPUCCINO. Step INSIDE WELCOME!

ANYONE COMING?

GUY WITH A BRIEFCASE, WOMAN WEARING NYLONS, WHITE SOCKS AND REEBOKS APPROACHING RAPIDLY FROM THE LEFT.

the Woman who does Everything More Beautifully than you never wastes a morning sitting around the Veterinarian's office.

Home, Home on the range... where the deer and the antelope play.

Wednesday: took SUZIE, LORD JEFF AND YEATS in to the Vet's. AS SOON AS SHE HEARD I WAS there, DR. GREAT-HART RUSHED out to EMBRACE ME... SHE INSISTED THAT THERE BE NO CHARGE FOR the visit BECAUSE MY PetS ARE SO ADORABLE AND WELL-BEHAVED, it's AN HONOR to treat them.

MORE BOOKS FROM

HYSTERIA

Getting in Touch with Your Inner Bitch
by Elizabeth Hilts $8.95

The Inner Bitch Guide to Men,
Relationships, Dating, Etc., Etc.
by Elizabeth Hilts $8.95

Women's Lip
by Roz Warren $7.95

Hysteria books are available at your local book
or gift store, or by calling 203.333.9399